In the Company of Spirits

In the Company
of Spirits

Poems by

CARMEN CALATAYUD

Press 53
Winston-Salem

Press 53, LLC
PO Box 30314
Winston-Salem, NC 27130

First Edition

SILVER CONCHO POETRY SERIES

Copyright © 2012 by Carmen Calatayud

Cover design by Solange Roberdeau
www.SolangeRoberdeau.com

Cover art, "In the Company of Great Spirits," Copyright © 2012
by Aydee López Martínez, used by permission of the artist.
www.aydeeart.com

Author photo by Ricardo Villalobos

Quote from "The Path to the Milky Way Leads Through Los Angeles,"
by Joy Harjo, used by permission of the author.

Quote from "The Other Side of Air," by Devreaux Baker,
used by permission of the author.

Quote from "From the Other Side of Night," by Francisco X. Alarcón,
used by permission of the author.

Printed on acid-free paper
ISBN 978-1-935708-69-8

For Ricardo and our beloved ancestors

Acknowledgments

Many thanks to the editors of the following journals and anthologies where these poems, some of which were earlier versions, first appeared:

Beltway Poetry Quarterly, "An Offering of Strength"
Borderlands: Texas Poetry Review, "Tale from Chiapas"
Breach Journal, "After Twelve Black Moons"
Cutthroat, a Journal of the Arts, "To My Father Juan, Who Thought There Was a War to End All Wars"
Delaware Poetry Review, "Hermana in the Sky," "Cave Walk," "Transfiguration between the Graves"
Gargoyle, "Soul Search in Mexico"
La Bloga and *On the Issues,* "Flames & Angels"(as "All That Is")
Más Tequila Review, "A Homeless Woman Speaks"
PALABRA: A Magazine of Chicano & Latino Literary Art, "Christmas in Las Vegas," "A Day in the Mayan Calendar"
PoetsAgainstTheWar.org, "Orange Crush"
Red River Review and *La Bloga,* "Border Ghost of Sonora"
Slow Trains, "Sea Lesson"

Anthologies

Cabin Fever: Poets at Joaquin Miller's Cabin, "Afterflood"
DC Poets Against the War: An Anthology, "I Fell Asleep Facing the Sea"

In the Company of Spirits

Location: BJ-24

ZWM.7J0H

Title:	In the Company of Spirits
Cond:	Very Good
Date:	2024-10-02 13:08:44 (UTC)
mSKU:	ZWM.7J0H
vSKU:	ZWV.1935708694.VG
unit_id:	18616733
Source:	GRISELDA

ZVW.1935708694.VG

delist unit# 18616733

XXXXX

We matter to somebody.
We must matter to the strange god who imagines us as we revolve,
together in the dark sky on the path to the Milky Way.

—Joy Harjo
"The Path to the Milky Way
Leads Through Los Angeles"

Ghosts

voices have spoken all night to me
rising from beneath water,

and I understood the language of
currents

that rushed and pulled their bodies
and was so anxious

to carry me with them.

—Devreaux Baker
"The Other Side of Air"

Tale from Chiapas

In this country, we count the trees, then count again.
We lift the streets by mixing paint.
Nine guardians live upstairs and we sing with them.
There's a slit in the sky and we reach through to pull down the sun.
We weave bluegreen patterns as we have dreamed them.
At times, tricky spirits swallow our eyes.
They bring bad news like the black moths.
We open the coffin, smell *el alma* during the wind.
We wait for angels in the cave.
Little stones line the path that measures nothing.
Trotting donkeys knock on doors to whisper the tale.
This voice is our constant companion.
We point to the northern sky before sleep smokes our limbs.
Fig trees spin into ash, and we wash our soil with milk.

To My Father Juan, Who Thought There Was a War to End All Wars

Valencia, Spain

The soldiers took your *Tío Rafa*:
dragged out of bed and shot in the street

the Franco way

the *Generalissimo* in my dreams
sucked away your soul
when they killed Rafael.

You and your friends played soccer
around the bodies,

death was a daily smell
and the sound of mothers who screamed
like hyenas

hung in the air.

All of this, this wasn't ordained by the Holy Ghost,
but an angel grabbed you by the *cojones*

and told you to go on.

Now you are gone and
I am sleepless inside this cave.

I can't see heaven
but sometimes feel its contents squirm.

It is wise to ask
who is my guide during these
wicked times?

Archangel Michael sticks his finger down my throat, and
now I have to tell your story.

*

Your country absorbed the chaos,
you passed it on through your chromosomes, and

I have this DNA of atrocities.

You didn't mean to thrash out your life
but there was the hurricane of war
and nothing to barter for food,

boxes of blood-red oranges
crushed in the street,

your face purple with rage.

I know you are wondering
how is it that Franco and George Wallace
are still alive
and still find ways to run this world?

At every turn you thought America
would make sense,

that hoarding canned food in the basement
would save us all.
I don't blame you.

Now all that's left
is to take what you told me and
transmute it for others

and yes, they have to eat it because
this memory is all I can serve.

Border Ghost of Sonora

In this corner of the desert,
she has already died.
I pick up her broken mask,
promise to glue it together again.

My mother roams the border,
floats between the countries
she thought would share her heart.

My pillow saves the dreams
the dead have weaved,
banking on *milagros*.

I have a monsoon wish:
Let the rains wash away
the boots of the border patrol
so they step in flooded sand

because I am tired of *la migra*
who walk with feet of rock,
who make me think that God
is a wolf in the night.

I string silver beads,
still believe in resurrections.
I get phantom pains where the barbed wire
cut my mother's arms.

My hair has grown into a broom
it sweeps away the blisters,
drags along my washgun hope.

Café con leche keeps me awake
in case of visions *de mí mama*.
She dreamed of dinnertime,
but I'm not hungry anymore.

I listen for her whisper:
it sounds like purple silk.

Low Rumble

for Michael Hughes, 1959-2011

There's no hiding from your empty bed.
Your carcass is gone.
Your spirit airlifted by the last chopper.

Across the way, a doctor tries to siphon gas
from your brain. He prays to your body
for answers as he writes the autopsy report,
his science no match for the machinations
you morphed into rocket man art.

Sell the watch. Sell the clocks.
I don't care what time it is
anymore. Your heavenly destination
waits but I refuse to mail your dust.
It's been weeks since you made
your way out of this world.
I bet you're sitting in Emerald City
with a frozen drink in your hand,
telling jokes to the Wicked Witch.
You know I kept hoping you would
choose the right pills and pop them
at the appropriate times.

Big flyaway moon, that's you.
Pieces of comet tail trail off after
you're gone. Chunks of stars
break and I imagine them
chasing you through the sky.

In another world, the helicopter that carries
your spirit lands next to the pyramids.
A thousand camels cross the sands.
Their low rumble reminds me of you.

Abuela's Eyes

Green-eyed trickster:
I saw you pick on your son
and he spat back until
the dining room turned into a
wet, Spanish frenzy.

A tinier woman never whipped up
such wrath. You were the matriarch
of blood-black veils and Valencian dialect.

You told me I was *bonica*.
I'll never forget.
But in your city of passion and palms,
across the plaza where brown-eyed boys played,
you raged.

I see you staring at me from inside
your white stone casket.
I wonder if you cracked a smile
before you blew your last breath.

Sometimes I jump when I catch my green eyes
I remember your fast mean Spanish words
and think: Marina Martínez,
you're part of the reason
I hesitate.

When I Learned You Were My Brother

time traded us around.
You're the warrior with silver eyes
& I'm your sister, flickering.

I ask about God
You blink
& the sky is pregnant with helium
We laugh ourselves to death.

To the palace we go.
I hug statues, you sculpt Noah's face.
I want to tell the children.
I brush against the place where angels live.

We hear sirens & smell heaven.

You were my brother before the ark
before crocodile rocked
before Nixon quit.

You were the stone beside the church
the lightening bug I put in a jar,
the silkworm that ate my first communion veil.

I don't know how to go back
so you teach me seven prayers.

Cigarette burns,
moon wails, lizard sheds his tail.

To see you in the dark.
To speak to you, divine.

Bracelet

Washington, D.C.

Marilyn Monroe tried to kiss me
like a bride smiling at the altar
when I drove past her mural at the liquor store,
but I wouldn't have it.

I was scared, so I turned around
and drove to the Lincoln Memorial.
It was night and the lights were on
so I thought I'd get inspired and remember
why I was born.

I walked to the wall and looked up the guy
on the MIA bracelet I lost as a kid and Major
James Jefferson he's still missing and I'm
bawling at the wall.

So I talk to the vet who's selling bracelets
and I'm his only customer, and I hear this
dried-out agony from inside his round chest
that could talk all night about a jungle
he never should have seen.

He says he was so scared in '69 that his
knees jumped up and down off the floor
and that he can't explain it, it was this
gut-awful fear you get when you know
someone wants to kill you.

I want to die with him and come back to life
in Illinois in 3010 and grow some corn and
ring the bells without worrying about
disturbing the peace.

I get wet on the way to my car with John
Rodriguez on my wrist and I tell John
I'm gonna take him away from this place
so he won't have to die in this city and
I won't have to die strange.

Orange Crush

Where you went it was
a thousand forests away
so I fell into the well,
gurgled your name
water-logged my heart,
drowned in the fear that you
were one of the disappeared.

Your name was on the list.
I begged the gods to let me touch your eyes,
sprinkle sun on your skin,
wrap my legs around you.
I was sure I could squeeze away the war.

I reach through the pines without reservation,
make my way along a peach-stained path.
Believe you are lost and want to be found.

There's no such thing as a corpse,
and seeing one they say is you
won't change that.

Here is an altar to call you back:
grapes and a bottle of Orange Crush,
a velvet chunk from your purple robe,
a deck of cards to pass the time.

Your photo breathes in and out.
It's close to puncturing the glass.
I take a breath to catch your rhythm
and suck you from the frame.

Hermana in the Sky

I can't scrape you from my mind
or fold up your altar.
You're the sister I fought for,
grief underneath my fingernails.
Your grace engulfed me,
took me over trails
where saguaros kept our secrets
and waved us by.
With you I was explosive.
I walked with fire and water.
Now that you're gone,
I attract tricksters *en mis sueños*,
step over carcasses,
run from fists flying
toward my mouth.
I dodge the lies.
I'm lonely for friends
like lightning
that strike my monsoon soul.

Last night I heard you weep
underneath my house.
Black bones cracked inside my throat.
You pulled me out of winter's cave,
but it's hell in the hallway
between guts and wisdom.
I'm tired of wandering
like a nomad. Aimless,
I wait for you to fly overhead.
Be my satellite. Show me where
to cross the border.
Haz la lucha conmigo.

Someone said that everyone
has a secret with God.
That secret is the time
we choose to leave and why.
I begged you to hide me in your grave,
away from saints who never respond.
Without you here, I punish myself
for the crime of chronic fatigue.
But I swear you're pieces of sun
that still work on me
from the southwestern sky.
You were strength without apologies
and left me to be average.
Dangerous, drunk moon.
I could suffocate on your speeches.
You commingled with the cause
and fell into night.

I wash away my days.
When I'm sick with sadness
I conjure your face on a stage of angels
then imagine you in front of me,
my wrists decorated in bracelets
to make you smile.
I don't have to tell you
that my lungs are filled
with tears. Too humid to move.
They breathe like clouds
passing by, waiting
for a gust of wind like you.

Commitment Otra Vez

for R.V.

Some generations ago,
you were a Zapatista
inside your great-grandmother's
womb, black eye sockets of
revolution, carrying roses
with the pink blown out,
dando gritos in earshot
of the Americas.

But now your doubt
is strewn across the room
like petals from dead *maravillas*,
even in this space you rent
where spiritual warriors
pray for your country
and you can finally sleep
through the night.

Listen, *amigo de los desamparados*,
this is your time, again,
beyond gut-level fear
and black and white film:
The explosions just keep coming,
and you are chewing on history,
and never let it be said
that all you could do was cry.

Flames & Angels

Washington, D.C.

There is misery by the busload. Mothers scrounge
for bits of bread. Children lose the race with flames.
We can't make sense of paper, rock or scissors
or velvet political games. We lose a day each night,
tending to the problems of the world in our dreams.
We can't help but contemplate this sinking earth.
We bulge with stories that don't belong to us. But
they are *ours* as much as they are *theirs*. The tribe
that is kicked & the tribe that does the kicking.
Far away, the border wall is a waste & the trails
overgrown. We pick our own pockets & chew on
chunks of grief. So if a cleaning woman gets run
down by the bus on 17th, awaken again. She is
us & *them* & *all that is*. This is your chance to run
head-on into angels & salvage some wings. There
might be a bus ride to peace. A way to put the fire
to rest.

Martyrs

God mercifully forgets us for a few hours.

—Nick Flynn
"God Forgotten"

The Letter I Wish I Could Send to Tia Rosa

Querida Tía,
You lived under so many black moons.
All the tempers, *Tía.*
Your mother who roared herself to death.
Your husband who smoked himself
to death. Your toddler son
who kicked you and pissed
on the living room floor.
You took care of them just as
lovingly as you took care of me.

You rocked me as a baby
and I know I howled.
Born the day after you,
another Pisces who cried an ocean
during our transatlantic calls.
You came in the winter,
brave to navigate this English-white world.
Your golden-green *ojos* merged with mine,
and I was taken by your tears.
You returned to your land
and left me without your olive arms.
I cried myself purple.
You must have seen that
life in America is cold.
You were smarter than us.
I begged you to take me
but you thought I didn't know
what your country meant.
I wanted to dance flamenco.
I wanted to drink *horchata.*
I wanted to be warm.
I knew the beauty
of my Mediterranean roots.

After you left, I prayed
to *Nuestra Señora de los Desamparados,*
abandoned to this American life,
an ocean away from you.
I would forget you for periods of time,
but not your morning voice.

You didn't call my father when *Abuela* died.
He called you to say we were on our way
to my high school graduation,
and you told him his mother was dead.
Ella se murió. His hyena screams, and me
paralyzed in my cap and gown.
You sent a telegram that came three weeks
too late. I spoke to you telepathically but
you were grieving too hard to hear.

I'll never forget when you saw me at 21.
You sobbed so hard at the airport
I was afraid you would fall to the ground.
But you were anchored in your seaside city.
You were the watershed who kept on giving,
vale la pena, you said. You brushed my hair
and pointed out the silver stars,
apologized for the heavy heat
and showed me avenues of palms.
The humid blue sky alchemized
into yellow kites on the coast.
Blood-red orange juice blessed
my throat and the blinding sweetness
made me cry. My heart exploded
because I loved the heat and loved you.
You were the saint who would never
get canonized, this is what my father said.

I am cold here in the United States.
I am fighting off a cold.
I am fighting off the memory of a father
who can't forgive himself for leaving you behind.
As soon as I get some money,
I'll come visit. *Te prometo.*

Arthritic Crab Cure

I'm a soft-shell crab
with cigarette legs that puff and snap.
I break my habits with broken teeth.
I'm grinding wads of sand.

I poke for details of my shell
I hear the cadence of claws
clapping in the waves.
I've tripped on the rocky extract
of my beat-up body before.

With cash in hand, I drag my plaster parts.
My aqua knees slam shut.
I'm shedding but want to record it
in Sanskrit instead of sand.
I can't let my gripes wash away.
I'm a crustacean with
crazy handwriting who can't
hold a stick anymore.

Option one: Become a sexy fossil
and wash away in a pose.
Option two: Become a collector's shell.
Sell me in a gift shop with seaweed
hanging doors. The glass shelf is
my habitat.

I scramble in the high tide
like the crabs you've seen before.
The salty water doesn't soothe,
it only chills my disposition
and carries me away.
I wake up frozen to a glacier,
waiting for an Arctic scientist
to find my petrified husk.

Radio as Savior

Came out of the womb
with a microphone in my hand.
I sing in Spanish with the radio:
Tus ojos son milagros,
tus labios llevan las palabras
de mi corazón.
To feel it in my veins
but I look nothing like my father
because I'm half-Irish martyr,
born to iron hankerchiefs
and imagine far-away green.

I listen to his Spanish rants
about *dinero* and the checkbook
that's always wrong, while Mom
sits on the pink toilet seat
as if it's a downtown bench.
Her place to weep and feed the doves,
avoid fists,
dream of the Irish Sea and
how many Spaniards drowned.

Doctor of the Rosary,
I want to be a saint,
a Carmelite nun who has
nothing to say.
I've become deaf to Gaelic,
find solace in Top 40 hits
like "Rock the Boat" and
"Love Grows Where My
Rosemary Goes."

But the radio in my head is
melting down, desperate for sounds
that belong to *mi gente* and me.

I run to Spanish mass, sit alone
with the misalette, crack it open
like a bright piñata to scoop out
the songs and learn them
under my breath.

With *la Virgen* in front of me
I inhale to swallow tears,
nail every single hymn
and squirm when Father Alejandro says
how lucky I am to be pale.

Sea Lesson

I've been sucking
sea waste from the floor
like a catfish on her rounds.
I've been chewing
on scraps of dialogue.
Now I listen to great big shells
& tiny pink ones, too,
and the tiny ones tell me a story
I can almost taste
& lick my lips with, and then
I'm muttering ocean words
to myself like silt, seaweed and algae turf.
I've been in this rocking chair for hours
watching you and you
swim by wise as flounders,
paying no mind to turbulence
from yachts and sharks.
My gills still weep
from time to time,
flap then lie still against my sides
& lose the desire to breathe.
I'm fingering foam
for the words to say
the waves tremble like a knee
holding back its reflex.
Without so much as a lifeguard's whistle,
the ocean's mouth slams shut,
& I'm left alone
drunk on salt,
chest filled with blurry prayers,
waiting to drown
and at the same time,
dying to know
oceanography.

Best Intention

To snuggle up with god and you
and the blue horizon on the other side.
No bloodshot eyes/no tough love.
Can't trust my mouth,
my ill-timed wild ideas.
I can't outrun the voices
that make me ask you secrets,
that long for you to pry me apart
as best friends do.
I'm sweating out the anger
& drooling with love at once.
Last night I moaned
like a moon out of gas.
Tried to sing myself to sleep.
The tea leaves in my cup mean
nothing. I tuck in the corners
& excuses. Excuse my prayers.
I want *tête-à-têtes* that break the dam.
So I dig through your underwear drawer
& smell. It's true: you're the salt
sucked out of the flood.
I'm still sniffing
when I realize you're better off
without my personal questions.

Losing the Ocean

The sea is my religion that brings me
to the bottom and this is what I know:

The fear of suffocation and the fear of joy,
the selfishness that fills my throat
and tonsils too big to fossilize.

This face of scars from fishing with the mouth
and always dropping the catch.

I'm afraid of love that chews hips,
trespasses liver, runs after hurricanes.

Past oceans become present day beaches
and it's too late, mermaid,
lonely woman
without breast stroke maneuver,
without oxygen song.

You are the mineral washed away.
You are the salt that chokes a child
in August.

Christmas in Las Vegas

Lack of confidence
has taken me
to so many nowheres
I've lost track.
I've been here before,
in a dream filled
with black jack cards
and plastic breasts.
The best I can hope for
is to find the camp—
a white polyester suit
on a guy with a comb-over
and a big cigar.
A Dean Martin look-alike
crooning in a lounge.
A woman with a beehive
donned in furs,
caressing her cigarette holder
with a miniature poodle
by her side.

It's Christmas Eve
and you're drunk
high on Vegas,
positive you'll hit 21.
I forgave your last coke binge
and came on this trip
to visit our friend
in the federal pen.
There's a couple
sitting next to us
who just tied the knot.
The bride is giddy
in her white lace.

This place is filled
with people who spill dice
across putting green tables.
I wander away
to a special room
where the rich dress up
to play baccarat.
The bouncer explains
the rules, but
all I want to know
is if the mob
is watching us
through those cameras
from a suite upstairs.
Yeah, they are, he says.

A couple tells me
how they saved
their money—
she's a teacher and
he's a cop—and they've
come from Pennsylvania
to blow their wad and
see if they can
hit the big time.
Down $3,000
they didn't have,
they go home broke
and begin again.

I've become
a bottom-feeder
who avoids my friends,
spends Christmas
in this strange land.
I can't feel the air
in this hotel room
on the 23rd floor.
Dandelions sprout
from the green carpet.
I hear my mother cry
inside her house.
She's forgotten
my name.
My father's voice:
¿Donde estás, nena?
Es la Navidad....
It's 4 a.m. and
you're not here.
I mark notches
on the wall
to measure my wait.

You get caught
counting cards
and put up a fight
as they escort you
off the floor.
They tell you to
never return.
But this city is filled
with casinos.

Las Vegas fills me with
el temor de Dios.
But you are full of
the know. Taken in
by free alcohol and
the ferocity it takes
to keep up the bets.
You should know better
but you're a shark,
blue-eyed, bored,
with nothing left
because everyone's
given up on you
except me.

You remind me
that the odds
are with you.
You tell me how
brave you are.
I wish for courage
from an eagle feather.
I pray for the power
of flight.

A Homeless Woman Speaks

McPherson Square, Washington, D.C.

When the lump in my chest
awakens with falcon force,
I begin the morning with
candlelight. I'm scared of rain
and switchblades.

Breath by breath I escape from this
plot and begin to heave through
another day. Footsteps, groveling,
brushing aside. Who knew that bones
could bend? If I move to Tombstone,
Arizona, is it acceptable to talk
with the dead?

Oh holy fear of squad cars and guns.
Oh holy need for water and rest.
Oh holy fight in Washington, DC,
let alchemical justice flow
beyond Rock Creek.

I lay my sheet in the park and sleep
with angels of the highest drunk.
Someone is fondled at 4 a.m.
Another is stabbed at 4:45.
Dawn is worse than the night.
I surrender to sleep in its lightest
form. I hear myself beg for coffee
in my dreams. Tell the Homeless God
it's the only prayer I know.

Disturb Morning Birds

girl you are lactating
        separating from dried up telephone lines
and there's nothing left but
the jubilation of rainwater drops
busting up dirt you watch him kick and
        your face, never painted, crossed off the list
washed and tired, ready to please the flat sea
of his heart that fizzles and goes so quiet
but you keep talking to his sleep
        disturb morning birds
shake shake shut up bend don't sweep clean
he can't collect your milk

Sweat for Venus

Tucson, Arizona

My heart sags
from starry nights
when I realize
it takes just a sip
to spark your anger.
I try to boycott
your bloodshot eyes.

I sweat with fear
on 4th Avenue,
poke my limbs
like logs on the fire
after you loosen
your grip.

You berate me
in front of a retail clerk,
argue to win
because winning
is proof.
I beg you
to cease & desist.

Out on the street,
St. Vincent de Paul
is collecting coins.
I collect stones
to mark your steps,
take wisdom
from burning sage.

I dream I stepped
in front of a train:
the shock of heaven
for an instant
& your voice
on the frequency,
dry from telling lies.

Settled under
the covers,
your skeleton
grows sharp.
I crawl from
the wreckage
without evidence
of my misshapen brain.

There's no energy left
to empty the trash
make a cross-country call,
let everyone know
that no,
life didn't turn out
as I planned.

I'm a lazy martyr,
the kind the pope
can't recognize.

You're the choice
I can't justify.
I'm filled
with excuses,
surrounded by
survivor angels
when you shove me
against the wall.

My ten thousand tears
make the dust weep
& then Venus breaks
out of the sky.
She promises me
her love.

My bones are
sewn together
& suicide races
around my bed.
I'm quiet enough
to hear sunflowers
pant from the heat.

I'm too depleted
to spit on you.

Two moons ago
I gave this story
to the desert floor.
All my mistakes
are recorded,
but my language
stays sacred.

I couldn't leave
until now.

Letter from Plaza Luna

I went to the plaza craving espresso shots,
flooded by dreams of caffeine.
I need a thick pen and a steady hand
to write this letter to you.

I fell for a blue dress and a sunlit church
the winter we almost married.
I fell for everything but us
when your tongue erupted
like La Malinche.

Hot lava singed my skin
at the turn of the century.
Volcanoes had nothing on you.
But to be scared of you is
to be scared of dinosaurs.

My fear stretches back to the time
when these plaza stones were laid,
when saints tolerated feral men.
I don't have the stuff
saints are made of,
but sometimes I pray
that God will salvage my tired face.
The cells of my skin
shed every day
and I can shed you, too.

In this desperate head,
I smack the salt off the index finger
you shake in my face
and brave the bridge to minimum wage.

Under bulging clouds,
I take the stairs to the exit
where hummingbirds flutter
as fast as a caffeinated gypsy
like me can run.

Walk with a War Zone Girl

El Mozote Massacre, El Salvador, Dec. 1981
for Rufina Amaya

You're a live wire hiding in a tree.

If we were in a different place and time,
you would jump into a pile of snow
under a winter solstice sun.

But we're here, now, where the yellow-stained
smoke makes it hard to know if it's day or night.
This dusk of heat brings me to my knees so
I can peer into your eyes, round and brown
like planets unknown.

In this moment we have one another and
the blackberry pools of blood in the dirt.

*

They call themselves The Angels of Hell and
come to this village to apprehend one man.
They decide that one thousand are in the way
and leave the people in pieces: Crushed heads,
cobalt tongues, legs turned to a purple sky.

*

I want to steal you away in a starship built
for two, to a land for girls where bedtime
features as many saints as you need.

If I could fill my breasts with fresh water
for you, I would.

You don't ask where we're going.
You squeeze my hand and when I squeeze
yours back, I soak up your sunflower strength.
There is no room to fantasize. It's time to come up
with a plan. Fog starts to clear and the smell of
savagery rises to our nostrils. All my synapses say is
to walk with you until we slip through a doorway crack.

Driving Miguel's Low Rider Across the Border to Heaven

Rancheras coat my throat
as I ride the starlit highway,
shop for a shimmering lane.
Before logic presses my chest,
I make a quick choice that
causes the car to careen.

I crawl in one of the four directions,
far from the grief that staggers
behind me and the mountain range.

The desert stills my body.
Mariposas circle the crash site,
as though I were strewn across Michoacán.

Buried *sentimientos* rise like hungry beggars.
My eternity swallowed and held.
México, your river is in front of me.
The exhalation of pain disappears.

Mariachis sing, pluck each note *con cariño*.
A trumpet so bright my insides smile.
Silver buttons on a black jacket blind me.
I release my seat belt.
Mi cielo, I'm finally home.

Beyond Language

this life
condemned
to oblivion

here nobody knows
nor will know

of the sea
we carry
within us

of the fire
we ignite
with our bodies

from
the other side
of night

—Francisco X. Alarcón
"From the Other Side of Night"

Afterflood

I slogged through lakes to get
beyond the highways.
Each curve turned into a situation
dying for attention and lace.
No, I can't drink.
My words were chunks of liver,
blasted by heavenly structure
but now my voice is butter.
Without soreness,
I sing to hold god in my mouth.
Even while hearts are nailed to the fence,
I hear the cadence of each beat.
Love explodes and is tender as an infant's shoe,
begs us to walk down the street
listen to the dead in the heavy rain,
absorb the stain of water.

I Fell Asleep Facing the Sea

Ninety-nine miles a sheet
I wait for the rain to end,
pray for the army to be covered in fog.
I step over brains in the sand.
Starfish are stiff with grief,
and the Holy Spirit sighs.

Bullets smack I hide nowhere fast,
hands search for an ocean god.
My soul smells like a fish
swims to the other side,
pretends to be underwater just to muffle the blast.

Being human isn't intelligent at all.
It's seeing your fingers
in the appendage pile,
dreaming of Aztecs in a stack of hearts,
curling the tongue to close the throat.

El yo de la guerra es amor
They say this on the radio.
Fishermen take cover
from bullet spray
and watch the coast collapse in two.
The dead hide under the bed,
cry black-eyed salty storms,
beg for *machetes* to finish them off.

Contaminated angels,
now we stand as guardians of graves.
I used to make *sopa de pescado*
for my family of nine,
when the cooking of our country
filled Jesus' mouth.
Fish filled our frying pans
and dough would rise like the waves.

Ancestors of Arizonaland

for Tucson

The sun teases with shadow sculptures
while orange blossom scent chases me down.

I cry at the death of another day.
It's dusk in the desert, coyotes
call their sisters and I respond with wails.

Mountains tremble,
bent on crumbling the border
between peoples blended
hundreds of moons ago.

Under pomegranate sun
and the signal it sends
I walk with the elders,
hear ballads blow from their windpipes,
see their hearts stitched
by fibers as bright as flames.

Their bones float in motionless heat,
sometimes clatter through Sonoran dust
remind me that mesquite dreams are real,
that history can't be washed away:
La cultura has painted this cornflower sky
a color permanent and wide.

Cave Walk

I know the carcasses. Certain sensation, flavor of face.

Tempered cave paintings, deserted cups and blades.

Hieroglyphic lullabies soothe the jagged wall.

Spoon sand in circles of life. Snake settles for the evening.

Women grow feathers, fly through volcanic ash.

Maps depict swirling nightmares of spirits who negotiate death.

Systems of lightning love, beauty between the lives.

I want the dead to bite the wind and knock me over twice.

Chest rises, howls coalesce under seventh constellation.

In this cave, I die repeatedly with a bell in every hand.

Dance of hips gives rise to spine, sliding in the cold.

I am the violet moon, bone of a thousand smiles.

The Holy Spirit Speaks

I've stepped all over your prayers.
See blue *corazón* in the road.
This is your asking,
in the voice of Cuba spilling out of a cigar box.
Rich tobacco mixed with sand,
then scrubbing the streets of Sacred Heart.
Throw away your dialect,
and eat it for lunch.
Needing beads and chants, trinity touch and go.
Tricky spirits joking in their habitat.
They comb wet dark hair.
This corner of the street
sings glory, painful dust.
In ironed sleeves, there's dry anticipation.
Gypsy vision hangs inside these crazy bells.
Cherries spill across the stones,
a gift from Gabriel.
Pits tossed inside the sack,
sack holding, sack redeeming,
working without a cross.
Everybody's baptized
by the sun and that is all.

Your Guardian Angel Speaks

When I was alive,
I set up plastic saints on the floor.

Now I peel skin and
hide it for you to find.
We used to be siblings
but I've become your messenger,
filled with the Sinai and flickers of harp.

I know the seeds you've planted.
Your fear of dark harbors,
your fast driving down fevered streets.

Let me remind you that you are divine,
even as you walk between
the dead and the disheveled.
Your carnival tales rest
safely in my arms.

Follow the tracks of the sky.
Hear my yellow, dusty voice.
Trust your bones.

Your god is not a seduction:
She's your spirit in silent sand,
a gentle refuge of love.

Found in the Yucatán

for Ricardo

This is how you found me on the wind:
derailed, awaiting the sound of a rusted bell.

I awaken next to Xaman-Há
and the tender salt of your tongue.

I recognize the song in your throat
and the language fast asleep on my lips.

When my voice fades to sand,
you call me a laughing apricot.

You offer love stories from the ruins,
smile from blood that belongs.

We swim through the orange sky
and sing to iridescent quetzals.

Show me yaxche, the tree of life
before I lose faith in the sacred.

You are my lush sanctuary,
surrounded by clouds of sweat.

Fill me with a promise of the pyramids
where you sleep with borrowed stars.

Free to weave the patterns
you saw your ancestors create,

handed down through their dreams to yours:
This is how I found you on the sun.

A Day in the Mayan Calendar

We stand at the ruins to breathe Yucatán air.
With this flower we wed and you sweat.
Your glow, my tears change our course.
I will love you for twenty thousand years.
You will love me until jaguars rule the earth.

Soul Search in Mexico

We still try to learn from this fractured habitat.

Open the body, read the inscription. It says:
"This is a humid country broken into corn."

Vapors rise from a tired ghost
who wrestles with mezcal at night.

Skull of sugar, arms of cloud.
Too weak to fling beating hearts down the steps.

To feed the sun and hear nothing from the stars.

Look for foam in the garden.
Always emotion throat over stem,
then devour beautiful air.

To hear one swan word that dilutes angst.

Everything dark, then born to earth and sky.
Spirits return to chocolate soil.

Unfinished dream, the small lunar stone
explains sand lost between fingers.

This place enormous, without a door.

The answer so long in coming,
asleep in bodies we haven't met.

Buying Back My Voice

> *A pearl goes up for auction. No one has enough, so*
> *the pearl buys itself.*
>
> —Rumi

To sell my throat:
decorated with ribbon,
hung in a window
for the highest bid.

Knotted muscles that long for a drink
surround a voicebox shriveled pink,
emptied of words such as *yes, no,*
not so much.

Saturday night shoppers stupified
into believing a throat they see
to be better than their own

imagine what they would say
with a new larynx,
free of phrases they've been fed
an entire life such as
Whatever you want.

This throat is not for sale
I hear my mind form this thought
and move to the counter,
quietly place a debit card
next to the salesperson's hand.

I swallow the solstice moon
and fill my neck with strength.
I buy my voicebox back and lift it
off its sterling silver hook.

Dinner for Two

If you were alive
in my soup,
I would eat you.
Scoop you to my lips
with a silver spoon
and suck you
through my teeth.

I'm rude and loud,
just like you left me:
Howling like a manic coyote
underneath a broken moon,
even in this restaurant.
My tongue clicks
like castanets.
Still can't take me
anywhere.

Damn this hot sauce choke
and the tears that coat my throat.
Nothing can rescue my taste buds.
They blazed away with you.

If I could slide you
down my esophagus,
I would. I'd beg you
to warm my belly
and never excrete
yourself again.

An Offering of Strength

For those who cross the border to survive

The marrow I suck spills out of
                              my mouth
          in a dark room where the floor
                    is covered with black grass
          and dying trees that have a story to tell.

This is the sorrow I couldn't share before:
                    The border wounds ooze inside of me
and I'm just a vehicle
          for the United States of Pain.

          But please don't be afraid, Nogales.
                    Dear Phoenix, create a river with your tears.
Ciudad Juarez, outstretch your hands:
          I'm with you 24/7.

My heart squeezes the news cycle that
          never sleeps.
                    My palms beat the drums that
                              crash the dance.
          My throat holds the chants
                    that vibrate prayers.

Mariposas raise the roofs of the suffering ones
          who long for food and a tender bed.

This transformation tastes like ether but
                    anesthesia fades,
                              and the hour of breaking open
appears as a white marble moon
          on an early November night.

Ancestors arrive and say
drink to the soul in the sky.

Your time is now.
Your voice pure, deserving.
You are one in a long line of spirits
with blood that blesses us all.

After Twelve Black Moons

I lived without breath
in a shack of my own creation
after generations of war.

Put a padlock on the door
so I couldn't get in,
couldn't get out,
couldn't write or talk
or spit in any language.

I took refuge in angels and
my lazy left eye that could
see what it wanted,
blur the world
into a somber fog.

Twelve black moons stacked
on top of one another,
one each month until
the pile toppled over,
fell into twilight wind.

This is how rugged months passed,
year after year,
until I dug out a cave
of my own.

Here, explosions fade into lower tones.
Truce creates its perceptible hush.

What Matters: A Life in Five Parts

I

What matters is getting sharpened, getting loose, getting liquid,
getting high.

II

What matters is lying on a fresh grave to feel death along the spine.

III

What matters is the graceful book and the words that make us stay.

IV

What matters is the grey matter, the heavy matter and the matter
of fact goodbye.

V

What matters is the wind and the weight of being alive.

Moving to the Land of the Dead

Where the dead loiter and eat blue tulips
is the land I'm attracted to.
Where green grass is purple
and the sky a convoluted rainbow,
where rest is redundant and the sun
is all that's needed to lift our lungs
for another breath.

Where the dead play for hours
and drink lemonade is the place
I'm drawn to. Where orange lips hang
from trees and bottles of singing potions
are left open till morning comes.
Where hibiscus is chewed like
bubble gum and the raucous pink petals
stain our hearts for the rest of heaven's time.

Where the dead still use ashtrays as
décor is the home I want to live in.
Where doves as white as a blizzard
fly in and out of windows to laugh
arguments away. Where sugar sprays
like gunshot stars so children
awaken to sweetness. Where peace
resides in the bark of trees
and the leaves never drop.

Where the dead weave silk for pajamas
they wear all day is the town I'm moving to.
Where sheep sleep all day and drink rioja all night.
Where poems by Bukowski pour out of angels'
mouths and torch the campfire that melts
every disease of the soul.

In the Company of Spirits

We write on walls, on floors,
on stained façades: the elders' wishes
and the visions of cousins still to be born.

Inside our heads, rain thunders
its way through the sky of grey matter,
signals the storm of wet, sparkling stars.

We scrawl letters into heavy words.
This primal language drips from our lips
while eagles screech near the door.

Spirits appear on the steps above.
Marigolds sprout from their hips that glide down the stairs.
They unfurl the path, restore the family flesh.

We move outside to listen to birds, and see
tricksters wind their way toward our tribe.
Witness the wolves who create a chain around us.

Olive trees tell us to settle down, there
is nothing to be done. A thousand clouds
cry inside my chest.

A guardian takes my hand and moistens it with soil:
This is the land you came from. There is no worry in this dirt.
You are the harvest of our desert trance.

Spirits: Aftermath

Purple flashes and ancestor skulls
fell from the sky all night.

The dream resumes under the sun.

Transfiguration between the Graves

Arlington Cemetery

I cup the flame in my watery palms.

This charcoal sky won't protect me from my grief.
I'm terrified I'll bloom wide open.

I want to take my nerves
and drag them from the mud,
prove the moon isn't mechanical
and worm away from god-sized lies.

I want to watch headstones dance and
collapse, and turn into the green smoke
I could never see before.

I want to sit in the broken rain.

I'm a shaky miracle, gargling fire and water.
I want chaos and beauty in one big bite.

I want to feel the sum of all my lives
and feel the zero before I was born,
because my hands are full of flames
and so empty the palm lines are gone.

I want to sweat without explaining
and hold my death for an instant.

I want to be part of the air that travels
between grave and sky,
that visits this city and brings flowers to it,
that filters the tired bones
above and below the ground.

I want to float unnoticed
and swallow myself
and wait for nothing like a saint.

Notes

(All words are in Spanish, unless otherwise noted)

GHOSTS

Tale from Chiapas
nine guardians—taken from the book title *Nine Guardians* by Rosario
Castellanos
el alma—the soul

To My Father Juan, Who Thought There Was a War to End All Wars
Tío Rafa—Uncle Rafa
Generalissimo—General
cojones—balls

Border Ghost of Sonora
milagros—miracles
la migra—Border Patrol, Immigration
café con leche—coffee with milk
de mi mama—of my mother

Abuela's Eyes
abuela—grandmother
bonica (Valencian dialect)—pretty

Hermana in the Sky
hermana—sister
en mis suenos—in my dreams
Haz la lucha conmigo—Make the struggle with me. (Note: This is
how some Mexicans and Central Americans speak of making
the dangerous trip across the border. Instead of "Make the trip
with me" they say, "Make the struggle with me.")

Commitment Otra Vez
otra vez—again
Zapatista—a follower of Emiliano Zapata, a revolutionary who fought for the rights of peasants and indigenous peoples during the 1910 Mexican Revolution
dando gritos—give shouts
maravillas—marigolds
amigo de los desamparados—friend of the forsaken

MARTYRS

The Letter I Wish I Could Send to Tía Rosa
Tía Rosa—Aunt Rosa
Querida Tía—Dear Aunt
ojos—eyes
horchata—sweet milky drink made from rice and almonds
Nuestra Señora de los Desamparados—Our Lady of the Forsaken
Ella se murió—She died
Vale la pena—it's worthwhile; it's worth the pain
Te prometo—I promise you

Radio as Savior
Tus ojos son milagros, tus labios llevan las palabras de mi corazón—Your eyes are miracles, your lips carry the words of my heart
dinero—money
mi gente—my people
la Virgen—the Virgin

Best Intention
tête-à-têtes (French)—a private, intimate conversation between two people

Christmas in Las Vegas
¿Donde estás, nena?—Where are you, little girl?
Es la Navidad—It's Christmas
el temor de Dios—the fear of God

Driving Miguel's Low Rider Across the Border to Heaven
rancheras—traditional songs of Mexico that draw on rural life
mariposas—butterflies
sentimientos—feelings
con cariño—with affection
mi cielo—my sky, my heaven (affectionate term)

BEYOND LANGUAGE

I Fell Asleep Facing the Sea
(Inspired by Claribel Alegría)
El yo de la guerra es amor—The ego of war is love
machetes—machetes
sopa de pescado—fish soup

Ancestors of Arizonaland
La cultura—the culture

The Holy Spirit Speaks
corazón—heart

CARMEN CALATAYUD's poetry has appeared in journals such as *Beltway Poetry Quarterly, Borderlands: Texas Poetry Review, Cutthroat: A Journal of the Arts, La Bloga, Más Tequila Review, PALABRA: A Magazine of Chicano and Latino Literary Art*, and the anthology *D.C. Poets Against the War.*

In the Company of Spirits was a runner up for the Walt Whitman Award, given by the Academy of American Poets. Carmen is a Larry Neal Poetry Award winner and recipient of a Virginia Center for the Creative Arts fellowship. She is a poet moderator for Poets Responding to SB 1070, a Facebook group that features poetry and news about Arizona's controversial immigration law that legalizes racial profiling. Born to a Spanish father and Irish mother in the U.S., Carmen works and writes in Washington, D.C.

Cover artist Aydee Lopez Martinez was born in Teocaltiche, Jalisco, Mexico, and her family immigrated to the United States when she was four years old. She was instantly drawn to the coloring books, crayons, and sketch pads her mother had purchased to ease her children's transition from the drastic relocation. Aydee's mother didn't know it then, but she introduced her daughter to a lifelong passion for the visual arts and a yearning to express herself via color and imagination, powered by rich cultural symbolisms and strong family values.

Aydee grew up in the community of Cypress Park in Northeast Los Angeles and graduated from Franklin High School in Highland Park. She received her Bachelor in Fine Art degree from California State University, Los Angeles in 1999 and is now a full-time professional artist based out of Covina, California. Her work has been exhibited throughout California, and in Chicago, New York, San Antonio and Mexico. She has been commissioned to paint works by such organizations as the Down Town Los Angeles Grand Performances; Latina Leadership Network (LLN); California State University-Dominguez Hills; Los Angeles County Supervisor Gloria Molina; and Pomona Unified School District, to name a few.

Her work has also been published in the books, *Contemporary Chicana and Chicano Art: Artists, Works, Culture and Education*; *Triumph of our Communities*; and *Chicano Art for Our Millennium*, printed by Arizona State University and The Bilingual Press.

Today, Aydee continues to work out of her studio in Covina and is active as a member of the Covina Cultural Arts Advisory Commission, whose mission is to expose the community of Covina to free public cultural art opportunities and awareness. You can see more of Aydee's art at www.aydeeart.com.

Gratitude

There are many people whose generous hearts have made this book a reality.

Thank you to the people who, early on, believed in me and helped me realize that poetry saves lives: Ann Darr (1920-2007), Michael Hughes (1959-2011), Beth Joselow and Silvana Straw.

Thank you to the poets and dear friends who read this book in its various forms, and offered feedback and inspiration: Mary Azoy, Sarah Browning, Yael Flusberg, Beth Joselow, Niki Herd, Joseph Ross and Silvana Straw. Thank you to all the D.C. poets, writers and activists: You make our city come alive.

Thank you to the California poets and writers who engage and inspire me from afar, especially Devreaux Baker, Nancy Aidé Gonzalez, John Martinez, Andrea Mauk and Diane Solis.

Thank you to the past and present poet moderators of the Facebook page "Poets Responding to SB 1070," which has blossomed into a larger, nationwide movement that calls attention to "Arizona SB 1070," the anti-immigrant law that legalizes racial profiling: Creator Francisco X. Alarcón, Elena Díaz Bjorkquist, Lorna Dee Cervantes, José Hernández Díaz, Andrea Hernández Holm, Israel Francisco Haros Lopez, Odilia Galván Rodriguez, Abel Salas, Raúl Sánchez, Hedy Treviño, Edith Morris-Vásquez, Alma Luz Villanueva and Meg Withers. It is an honor to work with you to share poetry and give voice to the immigrants, people of color and students who experience racism in Arizona and elsewhere across the country. You are a daily inspiration.

Mil gracias to Pamela Uschuk and William Pitt Root for choosing this book as the second one in the Silver Concho Poetry Series for Press 53. Pam, I treasure your feedback, devotion and kinship. Bill, thank you for being a superb editor and a guiding voice.

Thanks to Eric Cohen, Megan Lavery, Micheline Toussaint and Cathy Snapp for friendship and loving support on this path.

Francisco Aragón, thank you for your kind, unconditional support.

To Aydee López Martínez: I'm so grateful and honored to have your beautiful art on the cover of this book. Thank you for your openness and generosity.

To Solange Roberdeau: Thank you for bringing this book to life with your stunning cover design.

To Kevin Morgan Watson, the passionate publisher of Press 53: Thank you for this opportunity.

To my husband Ricardo Villalobos: Your editing, support and ocean of love have made all things possible.

CPSIA information can be obtained at www.ICGtesting.com
Printed in the USA
LVOW06s1047110813

347313LV00009B/693/P